MARY HAD A LITTLE LAMB

Written by
Adrian M. Hurtado

Illustrated by
Jayne Koontz

Mary Had a Little Lamb
Copyright © 2024 by Adrian Hurtado

All rights reserved. No part of this publication may be reproduced, distributed, or transmitted in any form or by any means, including photocopying, recording, or other electronic or mechanical methods, without the prior written permission of the publisher or author, except in the case of brief quotations embodied in critical reviews and certain other noncommercial uses permitted by copyright law.

Although every precaution has been taken to verify the accuracy of the information contained herein, the author and publisher assume no responsibility for any errors or omissions. No liability is assumed for damages that may result from the use of information contained within.

Library of Congress Control Number:		2022921053
ISBN-13:	Paperback:	978-1-64749-860-3
	Hardback:	978-1-64749-984-6
	ePub:	978-1-64749-828-3

Printed in the United States of America

GoToPublish LLC
1-888-337-1724
www.gotopublish.com
info@gotopublish.com

*Dedicated to all
my former students*

Mary had a little Lamb
In Bethlehem was born
And Joseph Mary's husband
Was there that early morn

Angels summoned shepherds
To go in one accord
To see the new born Savior
The Lamb, the Christ, the Lord

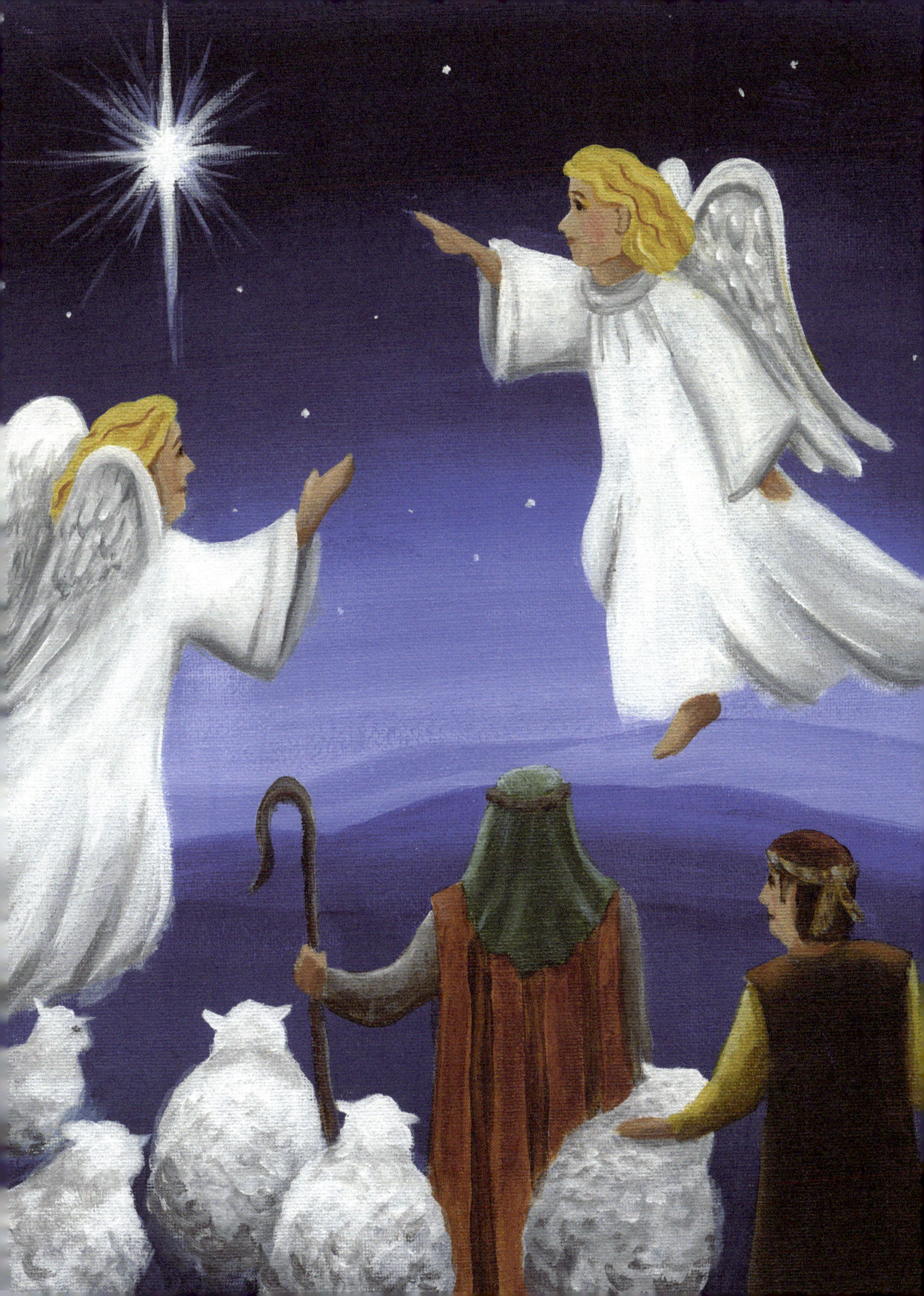

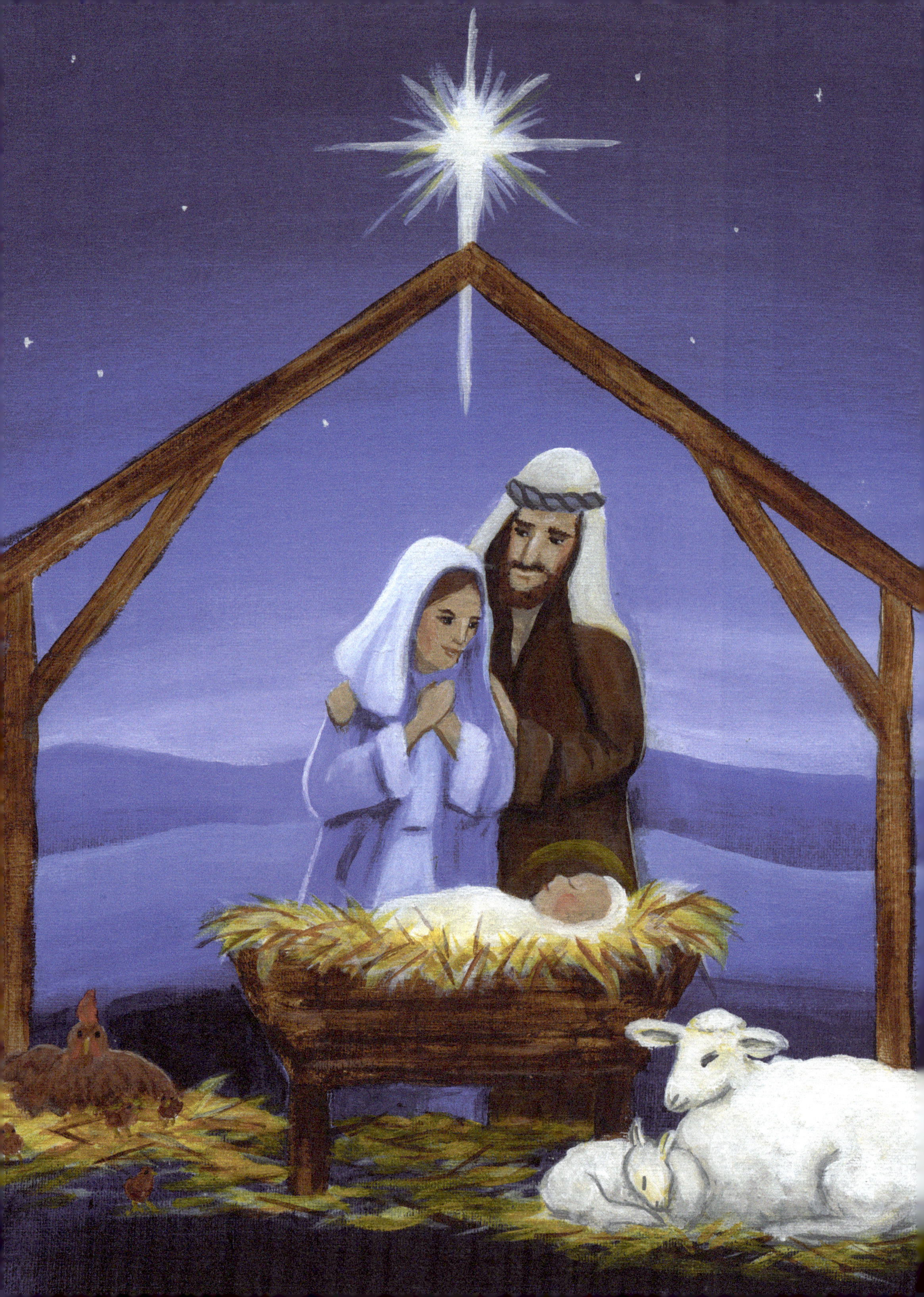

Wise men came to see Him
From the Orient afar
Guided in their journey
By a bright and shining star

Wrapped in swaddling clothes
In a manger lay the Lamb
And all gave praise and glory
For the new born Son of Man

King Herod of Judea
Was troubled by the news
For some proclaimed the Lamb to be
The new King of the Jews

Herod bared his anger
And in a jealous rage
Sent forth and put to death
Every male the new Lamb's age

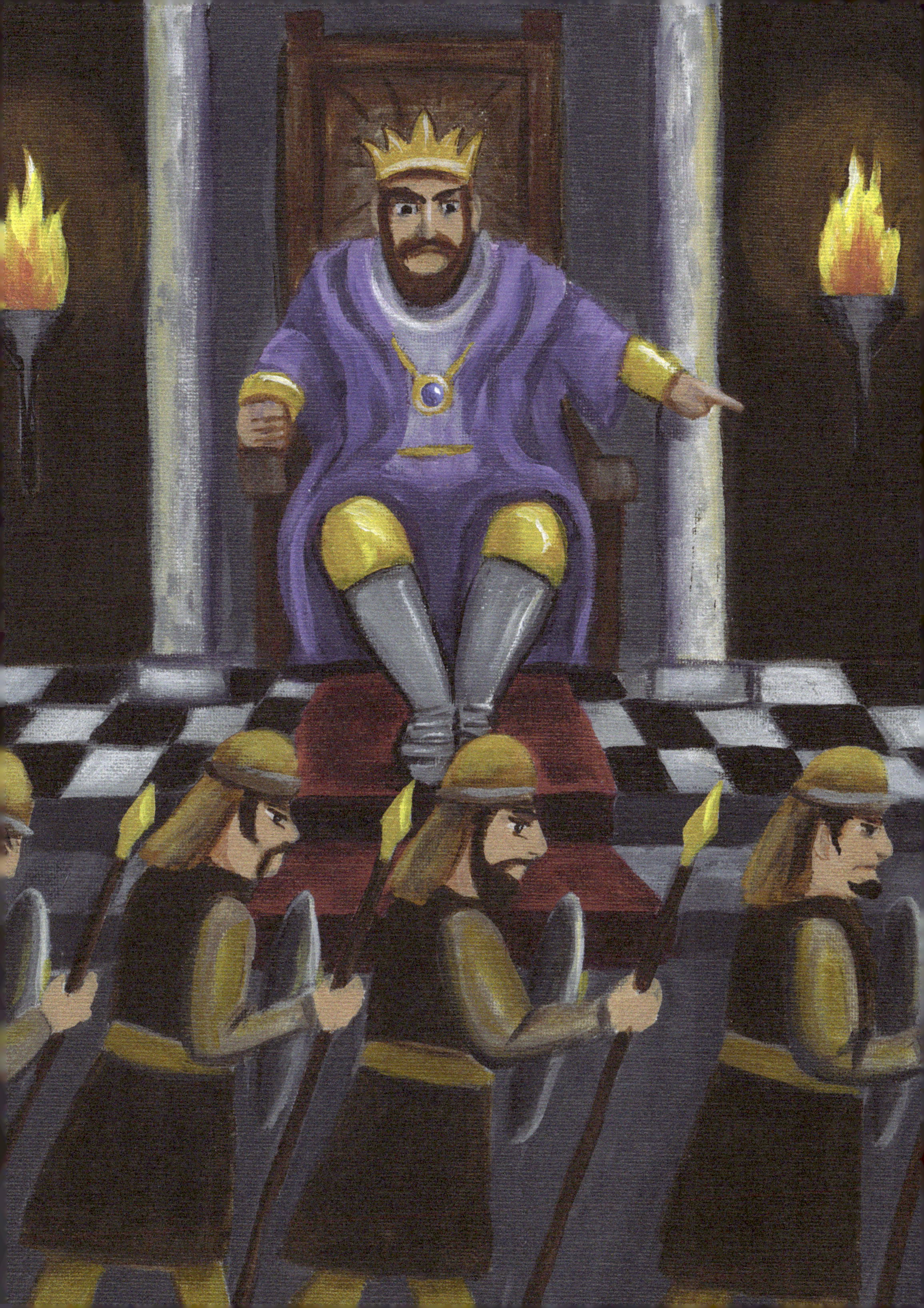

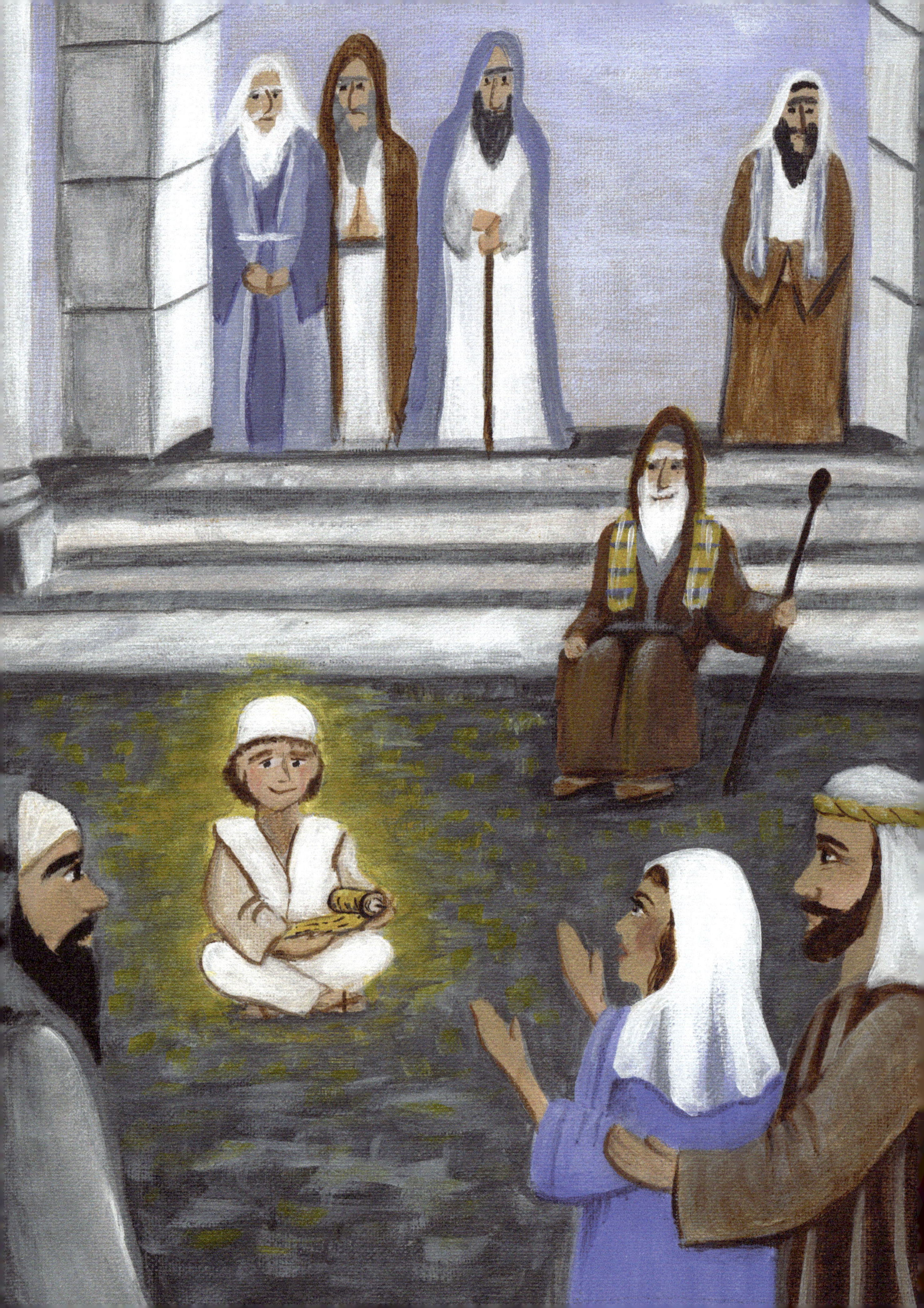

So Mary took her little Lamb
And into Egypt fled
Until an angel of the Lord
Announced King Herod dead

In Nazareth the Lamb grew strong
In wisdom and in grace
God's spirit was upon Him
All could see it in His face

When the Lamb was twelve years old
He strayed from Mary's side.
For three whole days she searched for Him
She found Him and she cried

The Lamb, amidst the teachers
Said to Mary and her spouse
You did not need to seek Me
I was in My Father's house

Years passed, The Lamb spent forty days
In the wilderness alone
The devil tried to tempt Him
To make bread from out of stone

But the devil was defeated
In the end chose to depart
The Lamb could not be tempted
For God was in His heart

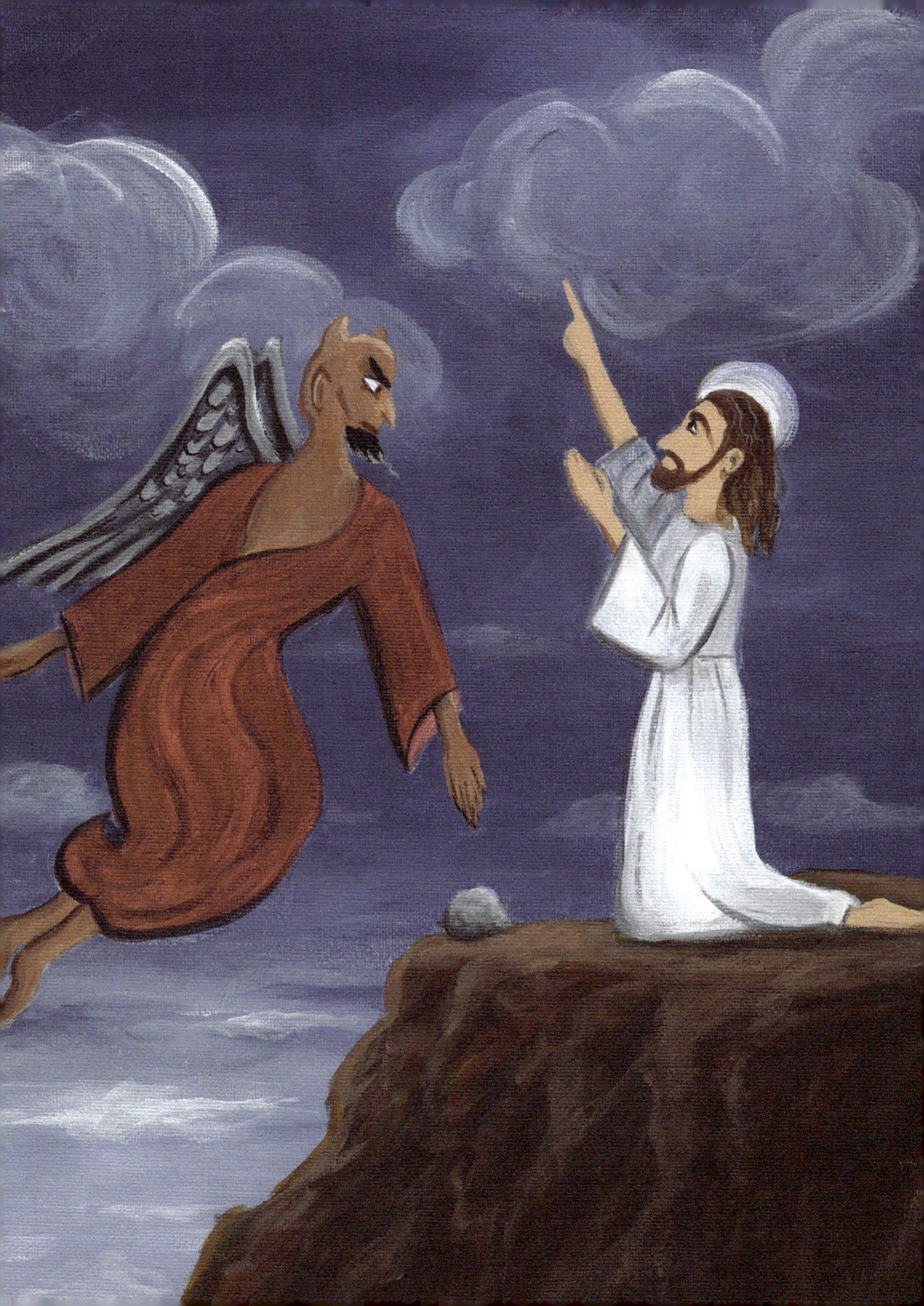

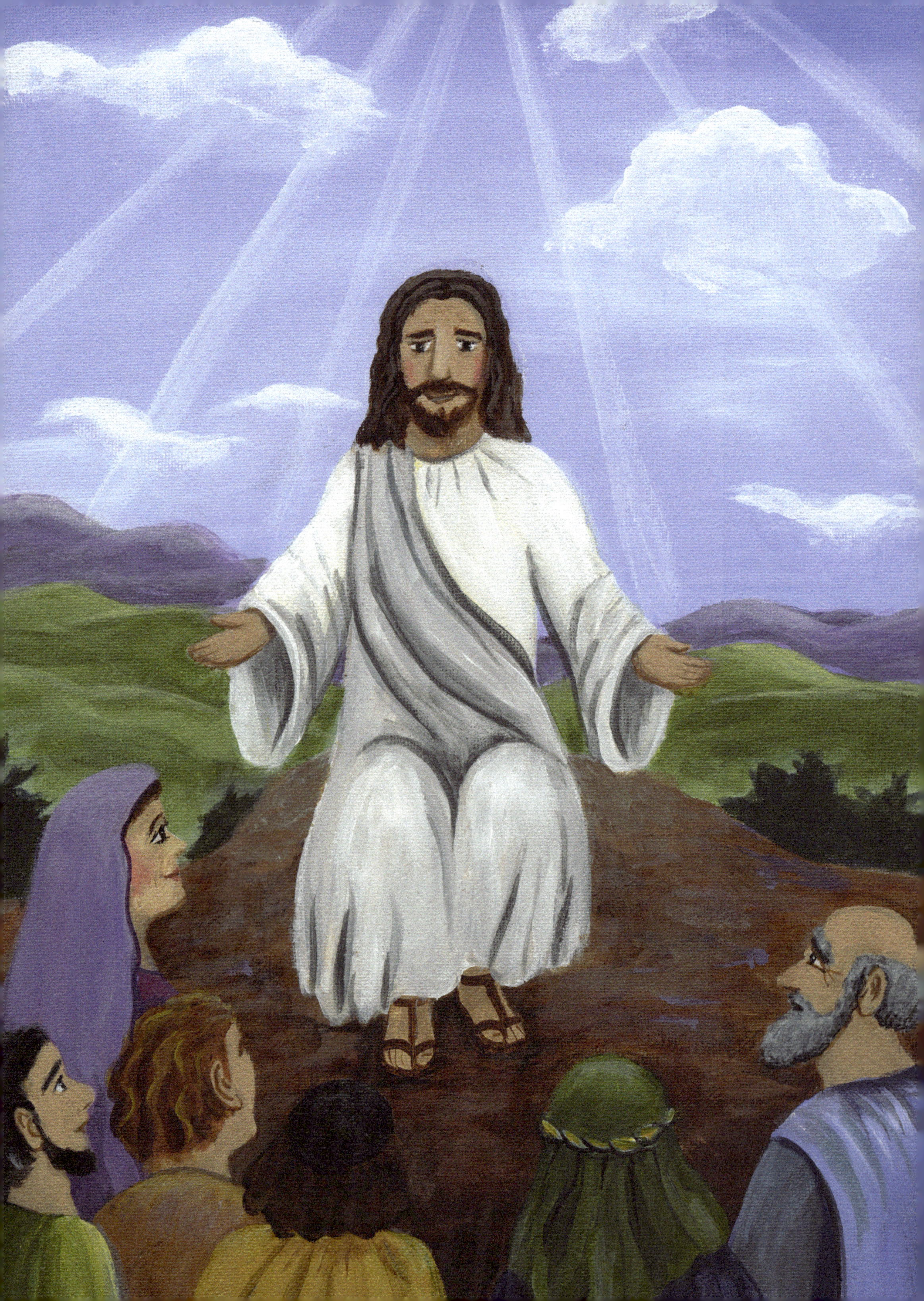

The Lamb began His ministry
Of God began to talk
The Lamb became the Shepherd
With mankind as His flock

The multitudes that followed Him
Were more than one could count
He gave them the Beatitudes
At the Sermon on the Mount

For three years more He walked the land
To spread the word of God
Through miracles and parables
A mighty work He wrought

The Shepherd Lamb taught right from wrong
And all He did was good
Yet some began to hate Him
As He had said they would

Then Satan entered Judas
And forced him to betray
The Lamb to those who hated Him
On Passover Day

The Lamb was in Gethsemane
He was there to pray
For thirty silver pieces
Judas kissed the Lamb away

Then those who hated cried out loud
Against the Shepherd Lamb
And turned their eyes to Pilate
To rid them of this Man

Though Pilate tried the Shepherd Lamb
No crime was verified
But still the people cried as one
That He be crucified

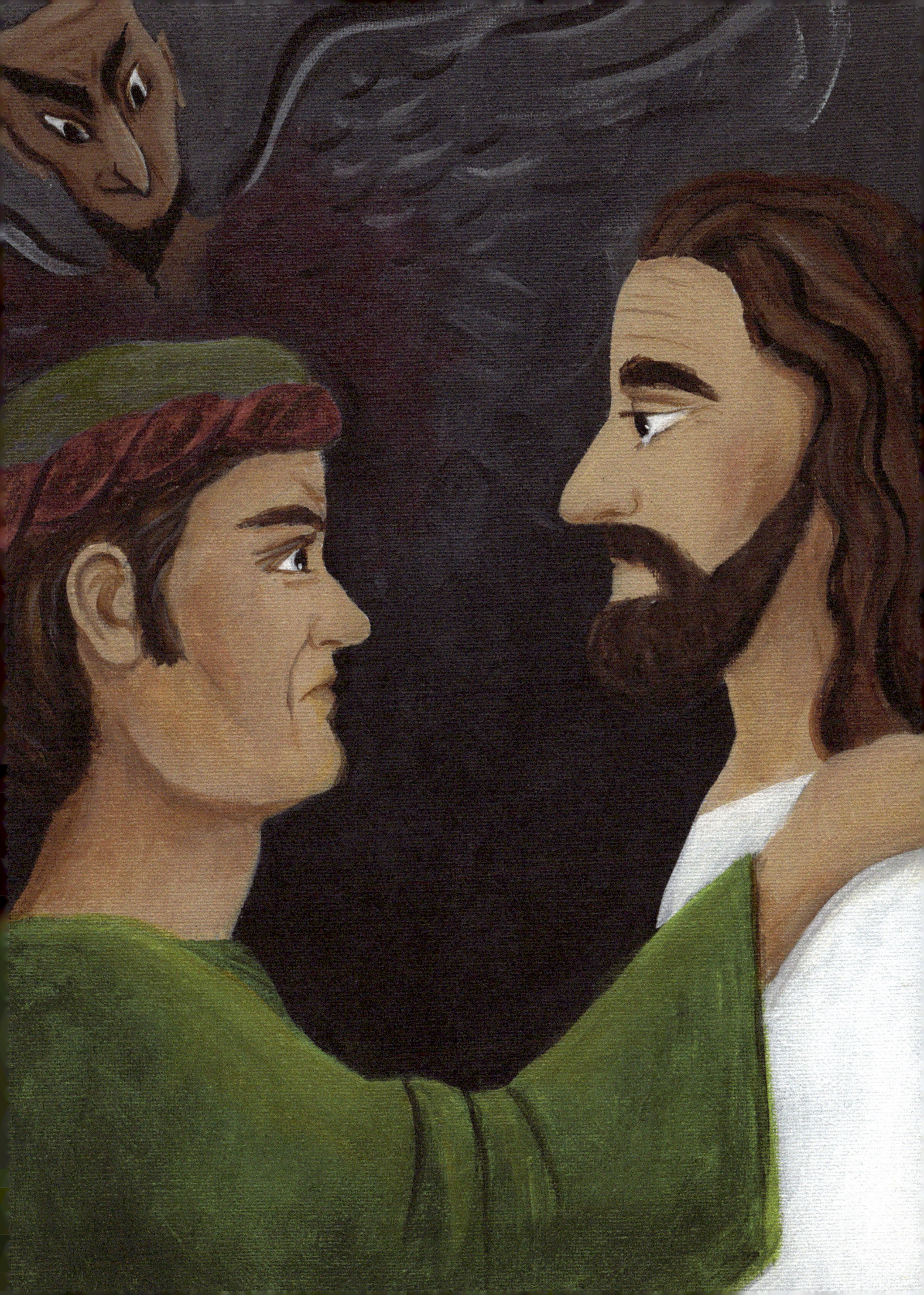

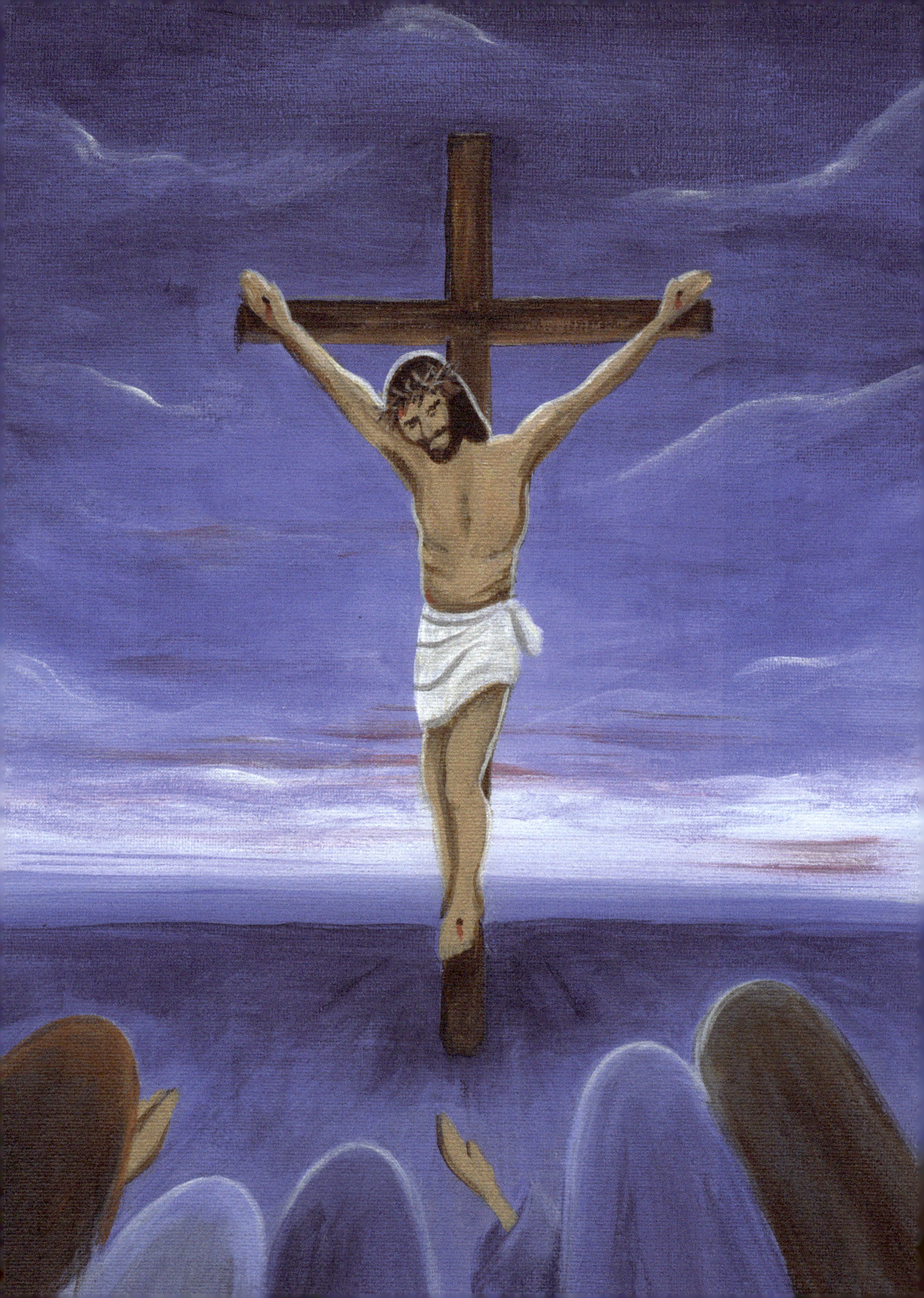

They stripped Him and they scourged Him
And beat Him till He bled
Then mocked Him with a crown of thorns
They placed upon His head

He was forced to bear the cross
On which He was crucified
And nailed to the cross on Calvary
He hung there till He died

Before the end He asked of God
Forgiveness for each man
The Shepherd Lamb knew He would be
The Sacrificial Lamb

They took Him down and buried Him
In a grave hewn out of rock
And rolled a stone in front of it
To serve as door and lock

Three days later He arose
To His disciples went
To bid them spread the Word of God
For this the Lamb was sent

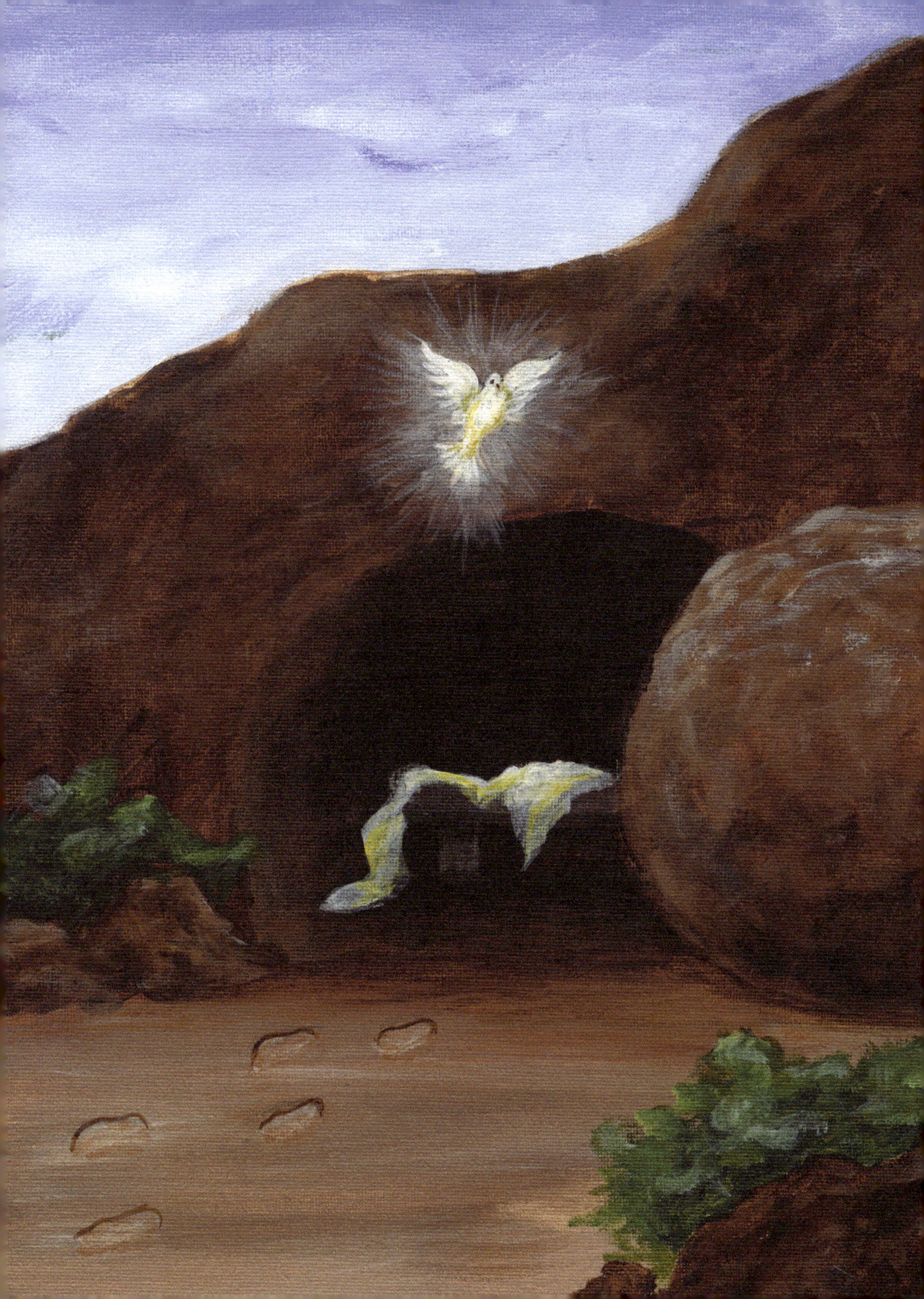

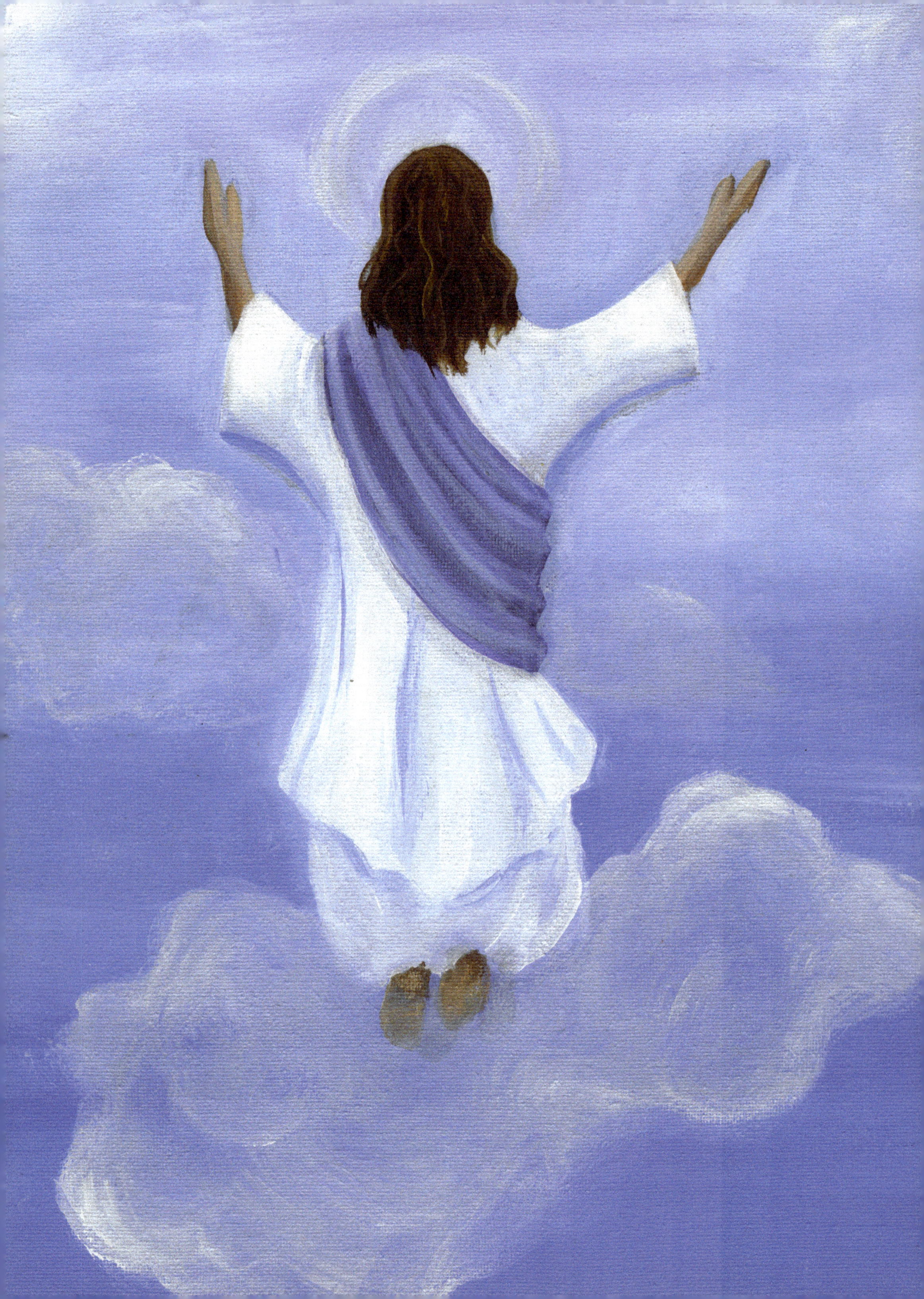

Then to heaven He arose
To sit at God's right hand
His flock gave praise and worshipped Him
To men in every land

And still today throughout the world
People seek the Lamb
For He truly is the King of Kings
The Christ, the Son of Man

For Mary's Lamb has no red suit
No reindeer and no sleigh
But Mary's Little Lamb is why
We have a Christmas Day

Milton Keynes UK
Ingram Content Group UK Ltd.
UKHW052304080224
437375UK00003B/105